by David Caudle

Dear Val –
Thank you so much for your
wonderful work and your awesome,
generous presence in the room.
Working on this with you has been a
joy!

Love,
DC

STEELE SPRING
STAGE RIGHTS

www.stagerights.com

VISITING HOURS

For all stage performance inquiries, please contact:

Steele Spring Stage Rights
3845 Cazador Street
Los Angeles, CA 90065
(323) 739-0413
www.stagerights.com

VISITING HOURS

PRODUCTION HISTORY

Visiting Hours by David Caudle
Weissberger Award Nominee; Premiere Stages Finalist, Named Best New Play of the Year by *The Times-Picayune*.

WORLD PREMIERE
RISING SHINERS at Mid-City Theatre New Orleans, LA 2012

Director – Ann Mahoney

Cast (in order of appearance):
SHELLY................................Jessie Terrebonne
NAT................................... Becky Allen
BETH.................................... Tari Hohn
MARIAN .... Becki Davis
PAUL...Nick Thompson

Stage Manager.............. Laura Jean Hoffpauir
Set Design.................................Roger Grissom
Lighting Design............................. Su Gonczy

FLORIDA PREMIERE
New Theatre, 2014 (Artistic Director Ricky J. Martinez)

Director – Margaret Ledford

Cast (in order of appearance):
SHELLY........................... Maria Corina Ramirez
NAT... Kitt Marsh
BETH...................................Madelin Marchant
MARIAN ....Barbara Sloan
PAUL...Alex Alvarez

Stage Manager..............Samantha Hernandez
Set Design...............................Alyiece Moretto
Costume Design .... Antoinette Baldwin
Lighting Design.................... Sam Deshauteurs
Sound Design .... Matt Corey

VISITING HOURS

PRODUCTION HISTORY (CONT'D)

ACTORS FUND BENEFIT READING, NYC, 2016. At HOWL! Happening Gallery, directed by Tony Torn, with Nick Ducassi (PAUL), Valeri Mudek (SHELLY), Deirdre O'Connell (NAT), Kim Sykes (BETH) and Kaili Vernoff (MARIAN).

DEVELOPMENT: Originally developed in Downstage Miami. Further developed in the Premiere Stages New Play Festival, Apartment 929 Theater Company and Torn Page Studio

Special Thanks: Andrew Block, Rem Cabrera, Stephen Chambers-Wilson, Hal Corley, Cyrena Esposito, Jane Friedman, Kate Hathaway, Laura Heisler, Angela Howell, Arthur Kopit, the Lark, Clark Middleton, Erica Nagel, Ethan Paulini, Tom Pelphrey, Laura Rohrman, Lisa Rothe, Eileen Suarez, Amy Wagner, John J. Wooten, Melody Fernandez.

VISITING HOURS

CHARACTER BREAKDOWN

Cast Requirement: 4F, 1M

SHELLY: Mid-30s (but passes for early 20s); a mysterious stranger.

NAT: 60; a wealthy woman in Coral Gables, FL.

MARIAN: 50s; Nat's friend and carriage house tenant.

BETH: 50; Marian's longtime Lesbian lover.

PAUL: 30; Marian's troubled adult son.

TIME

Summer 2010. The action takes place in one day, from morning to night.

SETTING

Primary Location: The living-room/kitchen of an apartment over a detached garage in the back yard of a posh home in Coral Gables, Florida.

Secondary Location: A jailhouse visiting area, which appears only once. It may be suggested simply with lighting and two stools.

Third Location: In Act I Scene 4, a separate spot of light should coexist with the living room set for the brief duration of one phone call.

RUNNING TIME

Approx. 1 hour & 35 minutes, not incl. intermission.

VISITING HOURS

AUTHOR NOTES

Visiting Hours explores the nature of love between parents and children, between romantic partners, and between friends. Love doesn't always heal. Marian's love for her son leads her into a powerful state of denial. She is not a gullible woman by any means. She simply cannot see what she cannot face. Beth's love for truth is at odds with Marian's need for fantasy. Nat's insecurities lead her to buy the love of her friends, but her love for them is clouded by her great need. Shelly and Paul truly believe they love one another. They truly believe they've both been wronged by society and are only fighting for their due. Shelly truly wishes she could become a part of this family unit. Paul takes Marian's love for granted, but on some deep level he longs to gain the love and respect of Beth. But Shelly and Paul are deeply damaged. The cause of the damage is unclear, and it's important that, for much of the first act, the depth of the damage is not apparent. Paul, in seeking Marian's help at the jail, displays all the qualities Marian needs to see. Whatever might be his words, he presents himself humbly, with remorse for past wrongs, and hope for his brighter future: being clean and employed. This may not be quite a deliberate deception. On some level, he truly wants to be the person his mother needs to believe he is. Marian, in questioning him, strives to act as Beth would in her place. She does an admirable job, forcing Paul to stay on track until he realizes Beth's influence may prevent him from getting what he needs. Shelly, in dealing with Nat and pleading Paul's case with Beth, keeps her cool and should appear more friendly than not, despite her words. Otherwise, Nat might call the cops, or Beth would see the extent of Shelly's damage too soon. Only after Shelly learns Paul has been released does she show her true colors, then reveal too much and slip into a sudden emotional spiral. Only Paul can calm her down. There is something stunningly powerful about the moment, but to anyone outside of their insular connection Paul and Shelly are incapable of giving. They can only take. And after they take all they can, only real love can repair the broken family they leave behind. After lashing out from pain and loss, Marian and Beth reach deep into their hearts and find their way back to one another. Even Nat shows that her love can be genuine and selfless.

ACT I

SCENE 1

Lights fade up on the living room/kitchen area of the apartment above a detached garage in the back yard of a posh home in Coral Gables, Florida. Mid-morning on a Saturday in early June. One door leads to the stairs outside, and the other leads to the bedroom/bathroom. A couple of small windows look out into the middle of a lush tropical tree canopy, which admits little outside light. Steps are heard on the stairs outside. A few knocks on the door. The knob jiggles, and eventually turns. SHELLY enters in skimpy jeans shorts and a crumpled top. She peers around the room, grabs a paper towel from the kitchen area and wipes the sweat off her face. She exits into the bedroom. NAT enters, a well-heeled, elegant woman carrying a gin and tonic in a tall glass.

NAT: Yoo-hoo! Hello?

The toilet flushes.

Marian? Beth?

SHELLY re-enters.

SHELLY: Are you Beth?

NAT: Why would I call out my own name?

SHELLY: I dunno. I'm kinda out of it.

NAT: How did you get in here?

SHELLY: It was unlocked. I'm waiting for Marian.

NAT: You have some business with her?

SHELLY: It's kinda personal.

NAT: Oh... well. I just glanced out the window and saw a stranger walking through my yard. That's my house in front.

SHELLY: Nice.

NAT: I think so. I'm Nat.

SHELLY: Shelly.

NAT: Shelly. Where does Marian work, by the way?

SHELLY: Don't you know? Barnes and Noble. Why?

NAT: Just making sure. Can't be too careful.

SHELLY: What if I was a robber? Were you gonna throw that highball in my face?

NAT: Hadn't thought that far ahead. Well. You must be their new project.

SHELLY: Huh?

NAT: We've all helped a stray or two coming out. Or fitting in. Beth and Marian might have the will, but not the means. Where'd you meet her? The church?

SHELLY: No.

NAT: Marian brought another young gal here from her church last year. Parents threw her out. This day and age, can you believe it? Anyhoo, I had 'em all over to the house for dinner, and it was like kismet. She was mature for her age. Sharp. She and I clicked for awhile, then we didn't. But I taught her some things, got her on her feet. You look hot.

NAT shuts the front door.

SHELLY: I walked from the Metrorail.

NAT: Good golly. How about a cocktail, hon?

SHELLY: No, thanks. I could use some water.

NAT: Make a lap.

NAT gets SHELLY a glass of water.

SHELLY: Sure is dark in here.

NAT: Yep. That ficus tree keeps this place nice and shady.

SHELLY: It's like the Keebler Elf house. What's the rent on this place?

NAT: My gals don't pay a dime.

SHELLY: Wow.

NAT: See, I guess you could say they're my project.

SHELLY: They've really got it made.

NAT: I'm the lucky one. That I'm in a position to help.

SHELLY: I need two thousand dollars.

NAT: I'm listening.

NAT brushes some stray hair out of SHELLY's eyes.

SHELLY: Stuffy in here.

NAT: I've got central air in the house. Let's go. We can talk business.

SHELLY: I better wait for Marian.

NAT: They could be gone for hours.

SHELLY: I need to be here.

NAT: We'll know when she pulls in. I've got a bell rigged up under the driveway. Come on. I'm dying to see those eyes in decent light. What are they, blue?

SHELLY: Green.

NAT: Lush.

SHELLY: What?

NAT: Lush. Word association.

SHELLY: Alcoholic.

NAT: No. I meant your eyes.

SHELLY: I know. I meant yours.

NAT: Where did they pick you up, hon? And why didn't they tell me? Hell, I can see why they didn't tell me.

SHELLY: Why?

NAT: You're right up my... alley. Does that scare you, sugar?

SHELLY: Not really.

NAT: Some people don't like the direct approach.

SHELLY: Are you being direct right now?

NAT: I guess not, if you couldn't tell.

SHELLY: Why don't you tell me what you'd want for two— three thousand dollars?

NAT: Talk about soaring inflation. Why don't you tell me what you need it for?

SHELLY: To help a friend.

NAT: A girlfriend?

SHELLY: No.

NAT: Do you have a girlfriend?

SHELLY: No. Are you gonna help me?

NAT: It's always a pleasure to be of service to a young sister.

SHELLY: I can give you that... pleasure.

NAT: I like pleasure. It's what it's cracked up to be.

SHELLY: So am I.

NAT: No, you didn't meet Marian in church.

> NAT leans in for a kiss. SHELLY stands rigid, eyes fixed and staring.

Something wrong?

SHELLY: Just do it.

NAT: Do what?

SHELLY: Your thing. Just do it.

NAT: Listen—

SHELLY: Do it, take it, fuck it, whatever!

NAT: Hang on, now!

SHELLY: What, you don't want it?

NAT: Slow down!

SHELLY: Are you backing out?

NAT: I don't even know you!

SHELLY: You said—

NAT: The day I have to pay for it, kill me! Just kill me!

> *SHELLY stares coldly at NAT for a moment, then turns her back to her. Confused, Nat hovers near the door, finishing off her drink.*
>
> *They hear footsteps up the stairs. BETH enters followed by MARIAN carrying a box of donuts.*
>
> *They are surprised to find NAT there, with a stranger.*

BETH: Nat? *(To Shelly)* Hello.

NAT: Don't you know this girl?

BETH: Can we help you?

SHELLY: You're Marian.

MARIAN: Yes. Have we met?

BETH: What can we do for you?

SHELLY: It's Paul.

> *The name is like a bomb dropped in the room.*

NAT: Paul!?

MARIAN: Where is he?! Is he alright?!

BETH: Is he here?!

SHELLY: He's in jail. For something he didn't do.

MARIAN: But he's alright?!

SHELLY: Physically, yeah.

MARIAN: Thank God! Thank you, God!

NAT: Hang on! Did you two leave the door unlocked?

BETH: What?

NAT: She said it was unlocked.

BETH: It doesn't matter.

MARIAN: Where is Paul? Where is he?

SHELLY: I... can we talk alone?

BETH: Nat, we'll call you later.

NAT: No! She tried to—

BETH: It's okay.

NAT: But she wanted me to—!!

BETH: Two years, understand? We didn't know if he was dead or alive!

MARIAN: Nat, please.

NAT: I'll be in the house.

NAT exits.

BETH: Okay, what happened?

SHELLY: She was being a little too friendly.

BETH: I mean, with Paul.

SHELLY: Those donuts look good. Boston Cream. Can I have one?

BETH: Help yourself.

MARIAN: I need to see him! When can we?

SHELLY: Actually, right now. Visiting hours go 'til one p.m.

MARIAN: Let's go!

BETH: Hold on, honey.

MARIAN: How can you—?!

BETH: We gotta know what we're dealing with first. Why was he arrested?

SHELLY: The lady pressed charges, but it was an accident.

MARIAN: What kind of accident?

SHELLY: They were arguing by the parking lot.

BETH: You were there? You saw?

SHELLY: I was waiting in the shade, but, yeah. The lady got... she stepped too close, and... he didn't hit her. She fell. But how hurt could she be? I mean, she was so short, she was practically on the ground to begin with.

BETH: Was she hurt or wasn't she?

SHELLY: Treated and released, she was fine. But she told the cops Paul hit her with the tile.

BETH: Tile?

SHELLY: You know, the Spanish ones, for the roof. There was a stack of 'em by the building. Paul was only gonna throw it—

BETH: Did he?

SHELLY: What?

BETH: Hit her with the tile.

SHELLY: No. I already said that.

MARIAN: He couldn't do that.

BETH: Then why was he arrested?

SHELLY: Well, he cracked her windshield, too, so... but that was before. That was what he was doing with the tiles. She tried to stop him and she just... fell.

MARIAN: Paul wouldn't hurt someone. Not on purpose.

BETH: Honey, how do we know anymore?

MARIAN: I know.

SHELLY: And I'm telling you.

>   *BETH stretches her back and winces.*

  Are you okay?

BETH: ...

MARIAN: Go on, please.

>   *MARIAN brings BETH water and a pill.*

SHELLY: I told the cops, he didn't do anything. I mean, except crack her windshield, which was, like, an eye for an eye kinda thing. But they believed that lady and her nephew over me. They're calling it Aggravated Assault.

>   *MARIAN brings a donut. BETH waves it away.*

MARIAN: Eat it so you don't upset your stomach.

SHELLY: So... we should figure out the bail thing.

MARIAN: When will they set it?

SHELLY: Yesterday.

MARIAN: What? Why are you just telling us now?

SHELLY: We knew you both were working, so...

MARIAN: We could have taken off! Where is he? Why are we standing here just... talking?

SHELLY: We just have to come up with fifteen hundred—

BETH: Whoa!! Not another word about bail, you got me?

MARIAN: Beth!

BETH: Not today.

MARIAN: But two years!

BETH: That's right. And now, he's where we can find him.

SHELLY: You mean—

BETH: Give us a minute. *(To Marian)* We need to talk to his lawyer. Read the reports.

SHELLY: I just told you—

BETH: We need to see how he is.

MARIAN: Couldn't we just go, you know, prepared? So, if everything looks good...

SHELLY: ...Yeah. Like I said, he's totally straight now!

BETH: We are not making this decision today. Period.

MARIAN: I can at least see him and talk to him?

BETH: Absolutely. We both will. Let's go.

SHELLY: Um... I haven't slept, in, like, three nights. Mind if I crash here?

BETH: Why? How did you get here?

SHELLY: The Metrorail. And walking.

BETH: Come with us in the car. We'll drop you off.

SHELLY: Where?

BETH: Home.

SHELLY: That's the thing. We don't currently reside at any specific location.

MARIAN: Oh, my God. Well... you'll stay here until we figure out what to do.

BETH: How can she—? Nat's pretty bent out of shape.

MARIAN: She has to understand, this is an emergency. Come on! We have to go!

BETH: I don't think it's a good idea!

MARIAN: You're not the only one making decisions!

BETH: Fine!

SHELLY: Great, thanks.

BETH: One of us should stay, then. Don't you agree that one of us should stay?

MARIAN: I have to see my son!

BETH: Of course you do, I'll stay! *(Softening)* Go on, go see him. Give him my— Tell him—

MARIAN: Are you sure?

BETH: I want you to see him. But that's it. Understand?

MARIAN: I do. And I know you're right. For today, I'll just see him.

BETH: Okay. Go on.

MARIAN: Where am I going?

SHELLY: The courthouse. Downtown.

She pulls a paper from her pocket.

MARIAN: Keys! In my purse!

BETH hands her the purse.

BETH: Slow down. Just take it slow.

MARIAN: Let me go! I have to go!

BETH: If you don't calm down, you're not driving. You got me?

MARIAN: Yes, yes! Yes.

BETH: Okay. Call me after you see him. Or before. Whenever. Call me any time. Be careful!

MARIAN hurries out. SHELLY and BETH eat donuts in silence.

SHELLY: This cream tastes a little off.

BETH: Have a glazed.

SHELLY: It's okay. I'm used to it now. *(Beat)* It wasn't his fault. You have to believe me.

BETH: ...

SHELLY: That lady was supposed to rent us an apartment. She took half of the deposit, but then checked Paul's background or whatever, and when we went back to pay the other half, she told us we couldn't move in. And she wouldn't give us our money back. Bust her for stealing, why don't they?

BETH: I'd like to call his lawyer. Do you have—

SHELLY: I gave the paper to Marian.

BETH: You don't remember the name?

SHELLY: I told you everything. Besides, it's the Sabbath or whatever.

> Beat.

BETH: I'll be right back.

> BETH exits into the bedroom. SHELLY looks for a garbage can. Not seeing one, she drops the napkin on the counter. Beth re-enters.

Okay, it's all set for you. I turned the a/c on. It should cool off pretty quick if you close the door.

SHELLY: That Mrs. Hernandez. She's the one who should be locked up, not him! ...It seems like you don't believe me. Oh. Okay, yeah. I'm an Al Fresco American. I crash around. Dorms, friends, after hours clubs. So? You live in somebody's backyard, over a garage.

BETH: It's called a carriage house.

SHELLY: Walking down the driveway past this, like, mansion and climbing these rickety stairs.

BETH: We like living here. It's quiet.

SHELLY: And dark. And free.

BETH: That's none of your business.

SHELLY: Okay, I'm sorry. It's just— I don't think you should take their word over mine because I don't have a condo on the Intercoastal.

BETH: Don't you want to take that nap?

SHELLY: Paul told me about all the bogus programs you guys put him through. Rehab, twice. Counseling. Fuckin' Job Corps. None of it did jack. Now he's practically completely straight except for a little pot once in awhile, and it's all because of me, because I don't like to pollute my body! He's even earning some honest wherewithal, because of me! Not some government-funded bullshit run by people who just collect paychecks and don't really give a flying fuck. Like those cops and those lawyers—

BETH: Listen—

SHELLY: —It was me! When nobody else could, I have totally made your son a much better, healthier person! Except for the chlamydia. Shit, I talk too much. That's my problem. Oh, well, no, I don't care that you know that. Yes, I probably gave him chlamydia, but he never even had any symptoms and neither one of us has AIDS or anything and these things just happen. I've been totally good for Paul, even though I'm only 23 and he's 30, and people think I'm his daughter all the time, because he looks so old from the sun. I'm the only one you need to talk to about Paul. The only one.

BETH: Does your family know where you are?

SHELLY: Nobody knows where I am. Not even when it's ten p.m. Nobody's hugged me today, either. I'm nobody's fuckin' honor student. There's no bumper sticker for me.

BETH: ...Hey. Come on. Please. Calm down, okay? It's all ready for you, just go lie down.

SHELLY: I won't be able to sleep without a shower.

BETH: Okay. There's a trick to the hot water. You have to turn it on all the way at first, but be ready to turn it about half-way back after a minute. Then—

SHELLY: I'll figure it out. I'm kind of an expert at strange plumbing by now.

BETH: Great.

SHELLY: My clothes are all pretty crusty.

BETH: I already put some out for you. They'll hang off of you.

SHELLY: I don't mind.

BETH: Great, well, it's all laid out. Towel, wash cloth, t-shirt, some sweatpants with a drawstring. Socks. I don't have any underwear that would fit you.

SHELLY: I don't share underwear. That's gross.

BETH: In that case, keep the sweatpants. They'll hang off you, but, like I said, there's a drawstring.

SHELLY: Thanks. You know, you're just exactly like Paul said you were.

> *SHELLY smiles at BETH and slowly exits into the bedroom, closing the door as lights fade.*

SCENE 2

Lights come up on the visiting area at the jail. PAUL, 30, and MARIAN sit in chairs facing one another.

PAUL is the picture of wronged innocence. MARIAN watches him carefully.

PAUL: That woman wouldn't give me my money back, saying I lied on the rental application. There she was, tryin' to look all innocent, and put upon, and like, pure little old lady. Old people are probably the least innocent of anybody.

MARIAN: Paul.

PAUL: Minute I started talkin' about the law, and my rights, she suddenly forgot how to speak English. That's two smoke machines she had crankin'— old-age and Spanglish. It's my fault she fell, I admit, but I didn't... I'm glad she's okay. What about you, mom? You okay? You... happy?

MARIAN: Happy? How did that girl know where we were living?

PAUL: She went to your old place and you were gone, and—

MARIAN: My cell phone number hasn't changed.

PAUL: I couldn't remember it.

MARIAN: My work number is in the book.

PAUL: She didn't want to upset you at work—

MARIAN: That's ridiculous.

PAUL: —So I told her to try Aunt Nat. She saw you guys comin' outta the garage in the backyard the other day and—

MARIAN: The other day? Why didn't she say something then?

PAUL: She gets shy at the last minute.

MARIAN: It doesn't make any sense.

PAUL: Neither does you living in Nat's garage.

MARIAN: The apartment upstairs.

PAUL: It's full of junk.

MARIAN: Not anymore. Paul, we had no choice. Insurance doesn't cover the program if you leave early. You knew that, didn't you?

PAUL: It was a hell hole.

MARIAN: At eight hundred dollars a day. Not to mention how much it cost to keep you insured in the first place. We maxed out all our credit cards, but we could barely keep up with the interest. We're lucky we didn't wind up...

PAUL: On the street? You can say it. It's not so bad, actually. Up north, I guess it would suck.

MARIAN: You could see Beth and me homeless?

PAUL: No way, mom, no way. But if I stayed in that place, they woulda killed me.

MARIAN: So you just disappeared.

PAUL: Seeing your faces after those quacks cleaned you out woulda killed me even worse. Besides, you were better off.

MARIAN: Never say that.

PAUL: I got clean on my own. For good this time.

MARIAN: How?

PAUL: I just... got sick of being an asshole.

MARIAN: I mean, just like that?

PAUL: Don't you believe me?

MARIAN: Nat cleared our debt just like that.

PAUL: Beth was okay with that?

MARIAN: Instead of rent, we pay a little bit back every month. No interest. And Beth sold her Hyundai, but it was a drop in the bucket.

PAUL: Shelly said she saw the Toyota in the driveway. I'm surprised you didn't sell that instead. It was new.

MARIAN: Beth said it loses half its value when you drive it off the lot, so...

PAUL: No, I'm glad. You deserve one nice thing.

MARIAN: You're getting too much sun.

PAUL: Not in here. Shelly and I have five-fifty. That was the other half of that stupid deposit. Total bail is $15,000, but—

MARIAN: I thought it was fifteen hundred.

PAUL: That's the bond. Ten percent. That's all you have to pay.

MARIAN: We should have been at the hearing.

PAUL: All they do is state the charges and set the bail.

MARIAN: But if you have family present— I mean, what was the point of all that sleuthing around? Unless—

PAUL: There was no sleuthing—

MARIAN: Maybe if the bail was low enough, you would've just...

PAUL: Mom. No.

MARIAN: What if you were never arrested? You'd still be gone.

PAUL: I was gonna call you. Even if this didn't happen. I was. I was only waiting until I got to the point where... After two fuckin' hard, messed-up years, I was probably about, maybe a week— one tiny little week away from calling you up to come over to my place for some KFC. Then this old— Mrs. Hernandez... treating me like a criminal. Land of opportunity. Right. It's a trap. They tell us anybody can be whatever they want in this country. Anybody, maybe.

PAUL (CONT'D): But not everybody. Imagine a country full of nothing but pop stars and billionaire athletes? Who's gonna drive the limos? Not me. Can't pass the background check.

MARIAN: If you want to change, you can.

PAUL: I already have. Shelly and I can pay you back for a third of the bond right now, if you put up the title to the Toyota.

MARIAN: We only have that one car between us. We can't afford—

PAUL: You don't give the car to them!

MARIAN: I know that... We'll talk about it tonight.

PAUL: We're talking now.

MARIAN: I mean, Beth and I will talk about it. You haven't even asked me how she's doing.

PAUL: Well, you know I wanna know.

MARIAN: She's fine. Well... her back is giving her fits.

PAUL: Still having pain?

MARIAN: "Discomfort." She threw her back out, moving a bag of charcoal briquettes. It was bad for a few days before she even told me. But I got her to a chiropractor, finally. They x-rayed her. It turns out, she grew an extra bone.

PAUL: Great. Her wish came true.

MARIAN: ...

PAUL: You used to like a little risky wit once in awhile.

MARIAN: She has pseudo arthrosis, an extra joint. It's a bone that grows from her spine, and attaches to her hip. It's rare but not unheard of. Makes her a bit more prone to back trouble than the average Joe.

PAUL: So... you gonna call her? Tell her what we wanna do?

MARIAN: It's not a conversation for the phone.

PAUL: Must be pretty sure she'll say no.

MARIAN: I don't know that, and neither do you.

PAUL: Shelly tell you? I'm— well, I was gainfully employed. Don't know now.

MARIAN: Paul, that's... What sort of work?

PAUL: Pools. Been helpin' out part time, puttin' in pools in Broward County. Hollywood area. Only part time, when they're short-handed. But it was starting to get pretty steady. If I can get out and get back to work now, I'll be okay. They'll keep me on.

MARIAN: I understand. I do. I'll tell Beth.

PAUL: Forget Beth for a second. What about you?

MARIAN: If I could only be sure...

PAUL: I won't disappear again? How good are you at memorizing? I'm working at Medallion Pools in Hollywood. On Johnson Street. The number is 954— I don't remember the number, but you can look it up. Call 'em. Owner's name is Charlie. Charlie was my reference for the apartment. He'll be my reference for the next one, too. And if it works out, he'll know where I live. Now. How can I disappear, when you know where I work, and my boss for sure will know where I live? Huh? Call Charlie. I want you to. He really believes in me. Could tell you I'm straight, too, since you don't seem to believe me.

MARIAN: I want to, I do, but—

PAUL yanks some hairs out of his head.

PAUL: Get it tested!

MARIAN: That won't be—

PAUL blows his nose into his hands and holds his palms out toward her.

PAUL: Look at that! Crystal clear. No blood. No nothing.

He blows it again.

MARIAN: Don't!

PAUL: See? Clear as corn syrup.

MARIAN: Don't do that again!

PAUL: Mom, I don't blame you. I was messed up when I left, I know that, but I'm different. Let me prove it to you. Like I wanted to, like I was just about to. Like you said yourself I still can.

MARIAN: This is not my decision alone.

PAUL: I'm your only living flesh and blood!

MARIAN: We both know blood is no guarantee! ...I'm sorry. But when you left, you must have known what that would do to Beth and me. What you knew your father did to you. No matter what happens, you know we want you home.

PAUL: Not what Beth said.

MARIAN: Don't lie to me, Paul. If you tell one lie I can prove, how do you expect me to believe anything else you say?

PAUL: Believe this. Shelly sees me as a "stabilizing influence" in her life. I like it. Mom, I can do it. I can work for a living and pay my own way and I can be a person in somebody's life. But Shelly ain't the type to wait around. I have to get out of here. Mom, Mrs. Hernandez already took my money, my home, maybe my job, some months of freedom. Don't let her take away my first crack at something like love... I let you have yours.

MARIAN: I'll talk to Beth as soon as I get home.

PAUL: No!

MARIAN: I'll make her understand!

PAUL: She won't! Goddamn! You just don't get it, do you? You're never gonna get it!

MARIAN prays silently.

That's it, pray! Pray for a fuckin' miracle! It ain't gonna happen! No self-respecting God's gonna perform a miracle in the age of Youtube!

MARIAN: What should I pray for? What do you need, Paul? What do you need that you don't have?

PAUL: The loyalty of a person.

MARIAN: Honey—

PAUL: The loyalty of any one human being.

MARIAN: You have that!

PAUL: THE FIRST LOYALTY...

MARIAN: Stop shouting!

PAUL: OF ANY HUMAN PERSON LIVING ON THE FACE OF THIS GOD-FORSAKEN EARTH!

MARIAN stares at him with helpless shock. Lights out.

SCENE 3

Lights up on the apartment. The bedroom door is closed. BETH flips through the newspaper.

BETH listens at the bedroom door. She quietly turns the knob and peers in. Footsteps are heard on the stairs outside. Beth opens the front door to NAT, who holds two cocktails and appears functional but slightly inebriated.

NAT: Figured you needed a drink.

BETH: That's not what I need. Shh.

NAT: She asleep in there?

BETH: Yeah.

NAT: I want her gone.

BETH: It's not like she's moving in.

NAT: Easy for you to say. You don't have a two-story house full of portable, pawnable goods, just sitting there like a duck.

BETH: I've got my eye on her.

NAT: You and what army?

BETH: I've got it under control. Just chill out.

NAT: Chill out? I could say the same to you, with those shoulders and that hair.

BETH: What?

NAT: Come on. A little G & T'll fix you right up.

BETH: I can't. I just took a muscle relaxant.

NAT: They only say that's bad to cover their asses.

BETH: I don't want it.

NAT: Hot in here.

BETH: You started early today.

> *NAT wanders the space nervously, eyes glued to the bedroom door.*

NAT: What did she tell you?

BETH: She told me what I needed to know.

NAT: I mean, about me. What did she say about me?

BETH: Just that you were friendly. Why?

NAT: She didn't try to tell you I molested her?

BETH: What? No, God. She didn't say anything like that.

NAT: I find that hard to believe.

BETH: Nat, she didn't come here to talk about you.

NAT: I want her off my property.

BETH: There are bigger priorities right now than your bruised ego.

NAT heads for the bedroom door. BETH intercepts her.

NAT: How long are you going to ignore the fact that she broke into this place?

BETH: What?

NAT: Did you leave the door unlocked when you left this morning?

BETH: No, of course not.

NAT: Then she picked the lock! I tried to tell you, but you were too busy sweeping me out of the room like yesterday's trash. I saw her walking through the yard, so I quick threw on some duds. Couldn't have taken me more than a minute. By the time I got here, she was inside. I think she'd already used the loo. You don't get into a locked place that quick without practice, and lots of it! That's what you've got sleeping in there! And who knows what else she's capable of! I do, that's who!

BETH: Nat, stop! She's just—

NAT: Just nothing! That little snake tried to charge me three thousand bucks for her... services! She expected us to do it, right then and there! I'm not making this up!

BETH: Are you sure you didn't... partially, maybe—

NAT: You bet your sweet bippie, I'm sure!

BETH: Well...

NAT: Don't you believe me?

BETH: Just wait 'til Marian gets back. What can she do when she's asleep?

NAT: What if she's not? Maybe she's listening to us.

BETH: You're paranoid.

NAT: Fine. She's Rebecca of Sunnybrook Farm.

BETH: By the time she wakes up, Marian will be home and we can all figure it out. Okay? Geez.

> *BETH goes into the kitchen area and starts putting dishes away out of the drainer. NAT sits on the sofa, drinking. The phone rings.*

Let me!

NAT grabs it.

NAT *(into the phone)*: Your dime... Thank you. For what? ...Oh. No, thanks. I don't care for Paris. That tower is ugly... Marvel schmarvel, I don't like metal. Look, can I just have the cash value? ...Fuck you, too.

NAT hangs up.

They say congratulations, and then launch into this pitch.

BETH: Next time, let me answer it, please.

> *BETH continues straightening the place. NAT trails her, sipping her drink.*

NAT: Times like this, you've gotta be sorry you ever got suckered into this mess. Thought he was gone for good, didn't you?

BETH: I don't see how I'm just supposed to sit here and wait, when Marian—

NAT: She'll be alright.

BETH: SMUGGLE YOUR PHONE IN, DAMMIT!

NAT: Jesus!

BETH: That's why she can't call. They hold your cell phone at security.

NAT: You gals shouldn't hafta know things like that.

BETH: I just keep picturing those tiny muscle spasms at the corners of her mouth. You know, when she smiles. Like, if she's happy, she must be getting away with something.

NAT: I used to find that little facial tic poignant. Now I think she should get it fixed.

BETH: When we were coming up the stairs with the donuts, she looked back at me. Just before she opened the door. Just for a second. There was that smile, just... quietly pulsating on her face. I thought, this might just turn out to be a good day.

> *BETH succumbs to tears. NAT rushes to comfort her. She is getting a bit wobbly from the cocktail.*

NAT: Let it go, honey.

BETH: I just want to be with her. Hold her hand.

NAT: And who holds yours? Who's with you?

> *BETH pulls away.*

BETH: Okay, okay, I'm alright.

NAT: I guess I'm out of a job. Whatever Paul's done, it must be pretty darn... I mean... what has he done?

BETH: I don't want to talk about it.

NAT: Maybe I'm thinking it's something worse than it really is.

BETH: I need to keep this a family matter, at least until Marian gets back.

NAT: I'm not family?

BETH: You just called it a mess. Now you want in?

NAT: I'm not in by now?

BETH: You are, but—

NAT: Just not immediate. I'm extended family. I guess that's why I'm always the one who has to extend myself.

BETH: Don't take this personally.

NAT: Well, you can't have him stay here.

BETH: Nat!

NAT: I'm sorry, doll. You and Marian might still feel the need to get him out of his jams, but I don't.

BETH: Nobody said—

NAT: Maybe I can't stop you from spending money on him that you've saved by not paying me rent. But I can at least say who is and is not welcome under my roof.

BETH: That girl will be gone, I promise! And he's in jail!

NAT: You really think Marian'll leave him there? You think she's capable of walking away and leaving him in there?

BETH: We agreed! Just let it go!

NAT: What, I don't have a right?

BETH: You have every right, Nat. But do you have to bully us about it every chance you get?

NAT: Bully? Where would you be today? This whole arrangement is exactly the way you wanted it. If anybody had a good excuse to go bankrupt, it was you two. I told you. Coast on minimum payments for a year, then file. But you were too proud for that. You'd rather owe your best friend— you'd rather jeopardize a real relationship, than alienate some anonymous— heavily-insured, I might add— corporations.

BETH: And now a day doesn't go by, you don't find a way to remind us.

NAT: How do you think I feel every day? I'm not blind. I see how you bristle when I enter the room. Even as you ask me to put in a word here, or extend a grace period there. Do I not do everything you ask? I keep trying to do more, to win you back, to savage our friendship. Salvage. Salvage. But the more I do, the worse it gets. It's too late, isn't it? The damage is done.

BETH: Nat... no.

NAT: Not damage?

BETH: We're obviously better off than we might have been. But... sometimes... it's true... it's... hard to see you.

NAT: Thank you for that. (*An awkward pause*) You're sure you won't partake?

BETH: I'm sure.

NAT downs the second drink.

NAT: You know what I think? Paul and I. We basically cancel each other out.

BETH: We don't see it that way.

NAT: No, you'd rather not see it at all. I'm sorry I can't just... spontaneously combust. Who knows? Maybe I can. I'll give it a shot. Get out of your hair.

NAT (CONT'D): Leave you everything in my will, and disa— you know, you're in my will, don't you?

BETH: Don't talk about this!

NAT: "Oh, don't talk about it. I hate to think of your gruesome, grisly death! Don't talk about it, please no, but don't spell my name wrong!" Yeah, I'll just leave it all to you two lovebirds, and disappear in a smuff of poke-pup— pup of smoke.

BETH: No. I just thought you deserved the truth.

NAT: The truth? You're mean when I'm drunk. *(Beat; struggling to articulate each word)* Now. I want that little uppity bitch out of here the minute Marian gets home. Whether or not you choose to post bail for Paul, I expect my monthly loan payment on time. And if he hoists his skinny ass on my property, I'll consider that tressspassing. Nothing personal.

> *With great dignity, NAT weaves toward the door.*

BETH: Nat. Don't leave like this.

NAT: When you tell a girl to get lost—

BETH: I didn't!

NAT: WHEN you tell a girl to get lost, you don't get to choose the road she takes.

> *She stumbles and spills her ice.*

BETH: Be careful!

> *BETH tries to take her arm.*

NAT: Leave me alone, I ain't kneewalkin'!

BETH: You're gonna break your neck!

NAT: No! Way to go, Nat. Some fuckin' exit.

> *NAT exits. BETH watches to see that Nat gets down the stairs safely. Then she gets a towel and wipes up the spill. Lights fade.*

SCENE 4

A while later. A spot of light comes up on MARIAN dialing her cell phone. The phone rings in the apartment.

BETH: Hello?

MARIAN: Oh, honey. I'm so sorry.

BETH: Are you alright?

MARIAN: Yes, are you?

BETH: Better now. Where are you?

MARIAN: I'm almost there. The Mobil Station on Bird Road.

BETH: Don't use your phone next to the pumps.

MARIAN: I think that's a myth.

BETH: Just come home.

MARIAN: How's Shelly?

BETH: She's taking a nap.

MARIAN: I'm so sorry.

BETH: Stop saying that. It's not your fault.

MARIAN: I have to tell you...

BETH: Honey, you're three blocks away. Come home. Tell me at home.

MARIAN: I'm not alone. *(Pause)* Beth? I'm sorry. I couldn't... I figured you might guess, when you saw how long it was taking. But I didn't want to just show up... honey? Please. Say something.

BETH: Thanks for the two minute warning.

MARIAN: He's off drugs. You'll see. I did the right thing.

BETH: Nat doesn't want him on the property.

MARIAN: He needs to be with people who love him tonight.

> Pause.

BETH: Then I guess you better bring him home.

> *The spot goes out on MARIAN as BETH hangs up, reeling from the news. The bedroom door suddenly opens. SHELLY enters from the bedroom. yawning luxuriantly. She wears Beth's T-shirt like a short nightgown.*

SHELLY: I love your bed. It's like laying on pound cake.

BETH: You look refreshed.

SHELLY: Thanks, yeah. That a/c felt great. Sorry to keep you out of your room so long... They're not back yet?

BETH: They?

SHELLY: I mean, Marian.

BETH: No. She's not back.

SHELLY: Oh, so—

BETH: Is that Marian's?

SHELLY: What?

BETH (*gesturing toward her mouth*): Looks like her shade.

SHELLY: I don't wear lipstick.

BETH: Oh.

SHELLY: This is just my lips.

BETH: Congratulations.

SHELLY: You don't wear it either, do you?

BETH: No.

SHELLY: You can totally get away with it, too.

BETH: I know what I look like.

SHELLY: Okay... So, was that Marian on the phone?

BETH: Yes. And, yes. Paul is with her.

> *SHELLY jumps up in triumph. The t-shirt rides up, briefly
> exposing her lack of underwear.*

Hey!

SHELLY: Oh, sorry. Didn't mean to flash you.

BETH: I put out those sweatpants for you.

SHELLY: It's too hot for that. I washed my underwear in the sink, but I didn't
see a blow-dryer, so they're hanging. (*Stretching the shirt down to her knees*)
Is this better?

BETH: Please go put something on!

SHELLY: They're still damp.

BETH: Too bad! You don't waltz around someone's house like that!

> *SHELLY exits into the bedroom and returns a moment later,
> lifting her t-shirt to prove she's wearing underwear.*

SHELLY: They actually feel pretty good this way. Nice and cool. I know you must
be thinking, like, who the hell is this chick, right? I know. It's not fair. I know
so much about you guys, and you've never even heard of me before today.
But I also know Paul. And contrary to, like, public opinion or whatever, I know
he deserves a chance.

BETH: He's getting one, apparently.

SHELLY: Don't you believe he can change?

BETH: I'm not going to discuss this with you.

SHELLY: I guess I have my answer.

BETH: 'Til now he wasn't hurting anyone but himself.

SHELLY: But I keep telling you he didn't— God, I sure hope the jury's more open-minded than you are.

BETH: I'm not his peer, I'm his parent.

SHELLY: Oh, wait, shit. Do you have an outlet somewhere?

BETH: There's a plug by the counter.

SHELLY pulls a cell phone and charger out of her knapsack.

SHELLY: Great. The battery's just about dead.

BETH: You have a cell phone?

SHELLY: Who doesn't? I'd go nuts.

SHELLY plugs in the charger.

BETH: How do you pay for that? Do you work?

SHELLY: I take donations for the cause.

BETH: What cause?

SHELLY: 'Cause I need money.

BETH: Is that what you were trying to get from our friend? A donation?

SHELLY: She offered. What am I gonna say, "no"? Then she took it back. She's a freak.

BETH: Don't try to talk around it. I know what you tried to do.

SHELLY: She's a desperate, lying old drunk. That's what you know. The minute I walk in, she starts making the moves on me. Telling me about the last little piece of ass you guys brought home for her on a silver fucking platter. Are you a pimp?

BETH: That was Marian's thing, she was trying to be nice, and when Nat horned in, we were both— this is none of your business.

SHELLY: Okay. Maybe you're not pimps. But just because people think they can do whatever the hell they want to me, doesn't mean I'm a whore, either.

BETH: You named your price, though, didn't you?

SHELLY: I'm so sick of this. People see me, they know I'm, like, a runaway, or at least I was when I was still young enough, and all the tired old scenarios start forming in peoples' heads. All those stereotypes. And it's all bullshit. Well, not all, I mean, yeah, my mom was too doped up on scrips to notice the "home schooling" I got from my step-dad. Why the hell would I want to look for it on the street?

BETH: You just said it. You need money.

SHELLY: Not that bad. I come into some major wherewithal from my grandmother when I turn twenty-five. Then I'm going to college. I'm just biding my time.

BETH: Who are your parents? I want to speak with them.

SHELLY: I'm not a child.

BETH: I have a right to verify—

SHELLY: Some parents' conference. A pervert, a pill popper, and a dyke.

BETH: So, you equate dykes with perverts and pill poppers?

SHELLY: As much as you equate survivors of abuse with crooks and hookers. It doesn't matter. You know, I actually used to think dykes had it made. Until I heard you on the phone.

BETH: I'm not interested—

SHELLY: Yeah. I never thought anybody with a pussy of her own could be so whipped. "Okay, honey, I guess you better bring him home."

BETH: I want you out of this house!

SHELLY: Hey, I totally get it. You need somebody to turn around and dump on. But it's not gonna be me.

BETH: Who the hell do you think you are?

SHELLY: I'm the only one that matters now. Because I'm the one who gets to decide if I want my baby to have two grandmas... or not.

BETH: I don't believe you.

SHELLY: Like you would know?

BETH: I know a con when I see one.

SHELLY: Are you so sure?

BETH: Why wouldn't you tell me sooner?

SHELLY: Maybe I figured you had enough to take in today.

BETH: When is it due? Answer quick.

SHELLY: Christmas Eve.

BETH: Perfect.

SHELLY: What?

BETH: That's why you suddenly needed a "nap." So she'd go alone. So he could tell her this without me around.

SHELLY: That's not—

BETH: Some "get out of jail free" card. Bravo.

SHELLY (*suddenly frightened*): That's not what happened! He doesn't even know, and you better not say anything! Shit! Bigmouth! Shit! Shit!

BETH: What kind of game are you playing now?

SHELLY stares blankly at Beth.

This must've been Paul's idea, because you've got to be the worst con I've ever come across. No smart answer? You know, I can see right through you.

SHELLY: No, you can't. You can't even see me.

BETH: Oh, yes I can. There you are. Right there.

SHELLY: Don't look at me.

BETH: "Look. Don't look." You run around here naked one minute and the next you want to shrink into the wall. Go ahead. Disappear. I'm all for it.

SHELLY: Don't look at me. Don't look through me. Don't.

> SHELLY starts to shake. She suddenly jerks her arms out and lets out a series of blood-curdling screams. She punches herself hard in the ribs.

BETH: What are you doing?! Stop it!

> BETH tries to grab her arms. SHELLY runs into the kitchen.

SHELLY: Stay away from me!

> SHELLY takes a bottle of Drano from under the sink. She tries to open it.

BETH: Hey! Paul's gonna be here any minute! They're only a few blocks away! Listen! Put that down!

> BETH tries to wrest the bottle out of SHELLY's grip. Shelly runs toward the front door. Beth blocks her path. Shelly locks herself in the bedroom. Beth pounds on the door as Shelly screams incoherently.

Open this door! (Grabs the phone and dials) Yeah, we've got a young woman here who's—

> The front door opens. PAUL rushes in, dropping his backpack. MARIAN follows, paralyzed with panic.

PAUL: Where is she?

BETH: In there!

PAUL: Put the phone down! I got it!

BETH: She's gonna poison herself!

PAUL: I said I got it!

> PAUL grabs the phone from BETH and hangs it up. As he bangs on the door, Beth picks it up again, ready to dial.

Babe? Babe? Open the door!

MARIAN: She locked it?

PAUL: What does she have?

BETH: Drano!

PAUL: Okay, this is gonna get a little messy.

> PAUL kicks the door open. SHELLY runs out, struggling to open the bottle.

Give me that!

SHELLY: Leave me alone!

PAUL: Drop it! Drop it!

> *MARIAN helps PAUL corner SHELLY in the kitchen area. Paul wrestles the bottle away from her. He hands it off to Marian, who holds it tight to herself.*

SHELLY: I don't want a human body!

> *She starts hitting at herself. PAUL pins her arms to her sides and hugs her.*

I don't want a human body!

> *PAUL quiets SHELLY and leads her to the couch. Beth hangs up the phone.*

PAUL: There's a good girl. That's not for drinking, is it? Nasty. Nasty, nasty junk. There's my good girl.

> *PAUL carries SHELLY to the couch and rocks her.*

Give me some water and a towel. There's a bottle of pills in my backpack.

> *BETH quickly pours the water as MARIAN gets a roll of paper towels.*

Tear one or two off. Dip 'em in the water.

> *MARIAN hands him the moist towel. He gently wipes SHELLY's forehead. Marian gets his backpack and finds the pills.*

MARIAN: How many?

PAUL: One. Now the water.

> *BETH hands him the water. PAUL lifts SHELLY's head tenderly. She takes the pill like a dutiful child.*

That's a good girl. Much better than that nasty junk. That's a girl.

> *He rocks her as she slowly grows quiet.*

That door is cheap as shit.

> *Marian approaches Beth. Beth turns her back. Marian folds her rejected arms across her chest as lights fade.*

END OF ACT I

ACT II

SCENE 1

Lights up on the apartment, a few moments later. MARIAN puts the Drano and other solvents and sharp objects into a paper bag. BETH watches her from a distance, still holding it all in. MARIAN's bustling activity appears almost cheerful.

BETH: Go ahead and whistle. I know you want to.

MARIAN: What's done is done. You can make it worse, or you can help me.

> *PAUL enters from the bedroom. The damaged door remains slightly ajar. Paul and BETH silently take each other in. This is their first chance for an actual greeting. They approach each other slowly. MARIAN instinctively glides between them.*

PAUL: Been awhile.

BETH: Right.

PAUL: Hear your back's out again. Lotta pain?

BETH: Discomfort. Some. You're getting too much sun.

MARIAN: That's what I told him.

PAUL: 'F that's the worst of our troubles, guess we're alright.

> *MARIAN guides them toward a possible embrace. PAUL pulls away.*

BETH: Your mother tells me you're clean now?

PAUL: My mama don't lie. So this is where Nat stashed you.

MARIAN: Stashed? No, honey.

PAUL: Got you chained up back here like a couple of rotweilers.

MARIAN: She offered us to stay in the house with her, but—

> *She looks at BETH and drops it.*

PAUL: She turn the sprinklers on you for sport?

MARIAN: You used to like this place. Whenever we'd visit Aunt Nat, you'd beg to hang out in here.

PAUL: Yeah, to play Indiana Jones. Huntin' mice in all that dusty old junk.

MARIAN: We got rid of the junk. And the mice, we hope. Rewired the electrics.

PAUL: It's still a dump.

BETH: Better than where you were.

MARIAN: Be glad you're here. We are.

MARIAN reaches out to hug him. He evades her and inspects the doorjamb.

PAUL: Probably full of termites.

BETH: Where did you think we'd end up, the Biltmore?

MARIAN: Beth, let's not—

BETH: He's here five minutes and he's already—

PAUL angrily slaps the doorjamb.

PAUL: You guys are here 'cuz o' me! Whadda ya want me to do, celebrate?

MARIAN resumes filling the bag.

PAUL: Geez, mom, you don't have to Shelly-proof the place.

BETH: What we need to do is call someone.

PAUL: No. Just let her chill out for awhile, she'll be fine.

BETH: She needs help.

MARIAN: If I just get rid of the, you know, booby traps—

PAUL: She's okay, I'm telling you. That was just... her schtick.

BETH: Are you kidding me?

PAUL: Where's the bottle?

MARIAN: Here.

PAUL removes the cap with ease.

PAUL: Trust me. 'F she wanted to drink it, none of us coulda stopped her.

BETH: What was that pill you gave her?

PAUL: It's for allergies. Not the medicine she needs, it's the ritual. Hardly ever happens, I swear.

BETH: How do you have a ritual for something that never happens?

PAUL: Hardly ever. What brought it on?

BETH: It's her schtick, ask her.

MARIAN: Paul, do you want anything?

PAUL *(ignoring Marian)*: I'm askin' you.

MARIAN: Eat? Drink?

BETH: Now that I think of it—

PAUL: What?

BETH: I told her you were almost here.

PAUL: Yeah...?

BETH: She had to know you'd be walking in.

MARIAN: Why would she—?

BETH: I don't know. I'm just saying, I don't think it was only for my benefit.

PAUL: Well, she'll be fine, now.

BETH: What about the baby?

PAUL: Oh, man.

MARIAN: She's pregnant?

BETH: You haven't heard this?

PAUL: No way, mom. There's no way.

MARIAN: Why would she say something like that?

PAUL: Who knows why she says anything? She likes to tell people she's deaf in one ear. She's an heiress. Her uncle invented Listerine Pocket Paks. *(Beat)* She can't have kids. Whole system's totally whacked.

MARIAN: How awful.

PAUL: Doesn't need a kid. She's got me.

BETH: Wipe that smirk off your face.

MARIAN: He wasn't—

PAUL: Hey. If it wasn't for me, she'd be... I see she plugged in her cell phone. She's had that thing since I met her. Don't know where she got it, probably found it someplace.

BETH: Yeah, in somebody's house.

MARIAN: Beth.

BETH: I know people lose their cell phones, but with the charger?

PAUL: Point is, she charges that battery everywhere we crash, but the phone's cut off. She can't call anybody, and nobody can call her. Even if they wanted to, which they don't. I'm with her. I take care of her. She doesn't have anybody else, and she doesn't need anybody else.

BETH: You're taking advantage of a very sad situation. That young girl—

PAUL: Older than I am.

BETH: What?

PAUL: She's, like, thirty-five, man. Damn. She really saw you coming.

BETH: What good does it do her to lie like that?

PAUL: Never had much good done to her, so I doubt she knows the difference.

MARIAN: The way you calmed her down. How'd you learn that?

PAUL: Had good teachers.

MARIAN can't help smiling.

BETH: Results aren't guaranteed.

PAUL: 'Cuz on me, it didn't take?

BETH: That's not what I—

PAUL: Shelly's fine.

BETH: She should be in a hospital. She's delusional.

PAUL: Delusional chicks are hot in the sack, though, eh? Praise Jesus.

BETH: You watch your mouth!

MARIAN: Both of you! Stop it!

BETH: Don't you get what he said about you?

MARIAN: Yes, and I won't fall for it. Paul, you get some humility right now, and thank the good Lord for giving you two parents that stick by you. Go on. Thank Him.

PAUL: Just tell him I said hi.

MARIAN: Go take a shower. You need one.

PAUL: Took one this morning. With ten of my closest friends.

MARIAN: You need another one.

PAUL: Great. I'm an offender, and I offend.

> PAUL laughs aloud.

MARIAN: Stop it.

PAUL: Where'd I put my backpack?

MARIAN: By the door.

PAUL: Everything's dirty, pretty much.

MARIAN: I'll take a load over to Nat's when you get out. There's a box under our bed that has some of your old clothes in it. They might be a little musty, but they're clean.

PAUL: 'Kay, thanks.

> PAUL finds his backpack, and goes into the bedroom.
> MARIAN looks in at SHELLY, then closes the door.

MARIAN: Don't worry. He hasn't let me touch him yet, either.

BETH: That's not what I'm worried about.

MARIAN: He's an open wound, Beth. Anything you say—

BETH: Stop making excuses for him.

MARIAN: He's not making any for himself. This is new. You heard him, he's taking responsibility now. He's been apologizing all day, in his way.

BETH: There are better ways.

MARIAN: Please don't confront him anymore, not—

BETH: Confront?

MARIAN: Not tonight. Tonight, let's just make him comfortable.

BETH: He shouldn't even be here tonight.

MARIAN: Honey, please—

BETH: I waited and waited by that phone.

MARIAN: I didn't go there with the intention—

BETH: How did he talk you into it? When she told me about the baby, I thought, no wonder. But apparently, that wasn't it. What was it? What made you think for one second he wouldn't run again?

MARIAN: He left that program, but he stayed in the fight. He got clean on his own.

BETH: If it's true.

MARIAN: I think it is.

BETH: Then that would mean he assaulted somebody sober.

MARIAN: He didn't do that. Beth, I asked all the hard questions. Watched his eyes. Did everything you would do.

BETH: I would have called you before.

MARIAN: It happened so fast.

BETH: No, it didn't. It doesn't. How did you even— what did you do, put up the car? ...Oh, God.

MARIAN: If I had called, Beth, would you have agreed?

BETH: We'll never know, now.

MARIAN: It doesn't matter. I couldn't have taken "no" for an answer.

BETH: I don't know what to say. *(Beat)* Did Nat see you walk up?

MARIAN: She didn't come out.

BETH: Maybe she's sleeping it off.

MARIAN: Don't worry. We'll make her understand.

BETH: I doubt that. She drew a trench in the sand today.

MARIAN: Why? How did it come to that?

BETH: She was drunk off her ass. Wanted to know the details. I didn't know what you'd want me to tell her, so I said I had to talk to you first, which I thought was our policy! She took offense.

MARIAN: You shouldn't have— well— She can't say no to me.

BETH: And even if she can... You can't take "no" for an answer.

MARIAN: Beth, that girl got to him. That means we can, too.

BETH: Your optimism turned to masochism ten years ago. By now I don't know what to call it. You put it in God's hands. So you can avoid the truth at all costs.

MARIAN: He spent the last two years thinking we never wanted to see him again. And if he'd been released without bail, we never would have. What would you have done?

BETH: I would have called you first!

MARIAN: You can't possibly—

BETH: Understand?! Because I didn't give birth to him?

MARIAN: No!

BETH: That's what it always comes down to! And you're right! I'll never understand that, will I? That bond? I'll never be a member of that club! That exclusive club, that only lets in the best of women! Like you! And the Virgin Mary!

> The bedroom door opens. MARIAN and BETH fall silent. SHELLY enters without a sound, looking at the two women as if they are statues in a museum, and can't look back at her. She now wears oversized sweatpants below the t-shirt. The oversized clothes make her appear even smaller and younger. She looks all around the room, then heads for the kitchen. Marian quietly hides the bag of "booby traps" under the counter. Shelly looks around the kitchen, then sighs.

SHELLY: There were donuts here...

BETH: I ate 'em.

> Jarred by BETH's voice, SHELLY stares at her, as if her eyes need to adjust to seeing Beth as a living person. Recognition finally sparks in her eyes, and she looks appealingly at MARIAN.

MARIAN: Are you hungry, honey? We have some pizza left over from last night. I could heat it up for you.

SHELLY *(softly, like a shy child)*: Donuts. Pizza...Okay.

MARIAN: I know, it's awful. We need to go to the store.

SHELLY: It's okay.

MARIAN: It's pepperoni. Is that...?

> SHELLY grimaces.

Take the pepperoni off?

SHELLY: Yes, please.

> MARIAN gets two slices of pizza out of the fridge and picks the pepperoni off.

MARIAN: I'll save these for Paul. He loves pepperoni.

SHELLY *(pointing to the pizza)*: Cheese.

MARIAN: Right. Now it's just a cheese pizza.

SHELLY: Scrape it off.

MARIAN: Oh... Okay. Like this?

> MARIAN pops what's left of the pizza in the microwave.

BETH watches intently from a distance, doing some subtle, contained exercises for her back near the front door. SHELLY eyes her with curiosity until Marian calls her attention back.

MARIAN (CONT'D): Don't like cheese, huh?

SHELLY: It'll still taste like pepperoni. Besides, I already had too much dairy for one day. The donuts. They had cream. I love it, but I shouldn't.

MARIAN: If you tell me you're on a diet, I'll cry.

SHELLY: Why? You're in good shape.

MARIAN: Yeah, well...

SHELLY: I think you're pretty.

BETH stops in mid-exercise. MARIAN briefly meets her eye, then looks away.

MARIAN: Oh! Wow. Haven't been accused of that in a while. Are you a vegan?

SHELLY: I don't have the discipline. But I am a vegetarian.

MARIAN: Must be difficult. I mean— where do you—?

SHELLY: I manage.

MARIAN: You probably eat better than we do.

SHELLY: Paul eats so much junk. I try to get him to have a salad once in awhile, but he just says, "Minute I start eatin healthy I'm gonna get hit by a truck."

MARIAN: That sounded just like him!

MARIAN chuckles aloud.

BETH *(with an impatient sigh)*: I'm going for a walk.

BETH exits. MARIAN starts toward the door, but the microwave beeps. Marian serves SHELLY her pizza.

SHELLY: Hot.

MARIAN: Oh—

SHELLY: No, it's good. Thanks.

As SHELLY eats, MARIAN takes a shoe box off a shelf.

MARIAN: Would you like to see what Paul looked like as a boy?

SHELLY: Sure.

MARIAN pulls photos out of the box.

MARIAN: Mmm. First trip on the Metrorail. Matheson Hammock park. Our old apartment. The one on Kendall Drive, not the last one.

SHELLY picks up one of the photos.

MARIAN (CONT'D): Oh. That's him at Coral Castle. Six years old. Pushing the big rock door open all by himself. It weighs something like nine tons, but it spins like a top. It really is amazing.

SHELLY: But it's torn.

MARIAN: His dad was in the picture.

SHELLY: Did you—

MARIAN: No, Paul did it. I told him he might regret it one day.

SHELLY: Not any day I can think of.

MARIAN: Has he talked to you about his dad?

SHELLY: Oh, yeah. About all of you.

> *Pause. MARIAN is both eager and afraid to ask another question.*

We saw you, once, in the Grove. You were showing Paul's picture to some people by Coco Walk. We passed right by, crossed Main Street, and just hid out in the library. He started taking these really deep breaths that were kinda loud, and clearing his throat. Everybody was giving him dirty looks, but he just kept drawing a box in the air with his fingers, and staring into it. I thought it was weird, but who am I to talk?

> *MARIAN fights tears.*

Can I see some more?

> *Grateful for something to do, MARIAN gets out another photo.*

What's this?

MARIAN: Easter. Same year. Anything, honey, anything, everything you think I should know...

> *PAUL enters with wet hair and no shirt.*

PAUL: Show and tell time?

MARIAN: I have leftover pepperoni pizza. Coming right up.

PAUL: Sounds good.

MARIAN: Sit down, then.

PAUL: What about you?

MARIAN: I'll wait for Beth.

PAUL: Where'd she go?

MARIAN: Uh...

> *MARIAN prepares the food in the kitchen. PAUL sits next to SHELLY and looks through the pictures with her.*
>
> *BETH enters. She joins MARIAN in the kitchen.*

PAUL watches BETH cross the room, then turns back to SHELLY and the photos. They laugh occasionally.

BETH and MARIAN whisper.

BETH: What's all this?

MARIAN: I guess dinner started happening. Paul wanted to wait for you. I didn't know... Look at them.

MARIAN massages BETH's shoulders.

So tight.

BETH: Don't, it's okay.

MARIAN: I ought to. These knots have my name on them.

BETH picks up MARIAN's purse.

BETH: Are the keys in here?

MARIAN: Yes. Why?

BETH hides the purse under the sink.

BETH: Just let me do this. It'll make me feel better.

MARIAN: Alright, but I really don't think—

BETH: I know. And I hope you're right. I really do.

MARIAN: You'll see.

BETH *(gently)*: Just please don't get your hopes up too high.

MARIAN: What good are low hopes?

The microwave beeps. MARIAN brings the pizza to the coffee table. PAUL grabs a slice as Marian sits next to him. BETH joins them with a cup of yogurt. SHELLY gets another photo and laughs.

SHELLY: What is that? A costume?

MARIAN: Oh, this, Beth, look! *(To Shelly)* That was the first time I introduced them to each other. We met for dinner at Joe's Stone Crab. Paul knew he was going to meet someone very special to me, and he insisted on dressing himself for the occasion.

SHELLY: How old was he?

MARIAN: Not quite eleven.

SHELLY: Awww...

MARIAN: First, he wanted to shave, but—

SHELLY: Shave?

PAUL: I did not.

MARIAN: Yes, you did, you wanted me to go out and buy you a razor, but I said, "You're too young."

SHELLY: That's hilarious.

MARIAN: So he stomped around in a snit for awhile, until I said that if he shaved, Beth wouldn't see his beard and know what a big man he was. So he let that go. Then he dressed himself in all his favorite clothes, whether they looked good together or not. Green corduroys, yellow Izod shirt and that red wind breaker. He looked like an oversized parrot.

SHELLY: Too many wardrobe options. We don't have that problem now.

MARIAN: When Beth first set eyes on him, at the restaurant, her first words to him were, "Nice threads." She couldn't have said anything better. And of all people, Cher was sitting two tables away, with her son from that Allman brother. She looked right at Paul and smiled. Twice.

BETH: That's right.

SHELLY: Wow. That's, like, a royal blessing or something.

PAUL: And at her next concert, she was wearing a seriously abbreviated version of my outfit.

MARIAN: As soon as we had a moment... Beth, tell them what you said.

PAUL: Don't put her on the spot.

BETH: No, she's right. You looked me in the eye and declared that it was "okay by you" that I was a woman. I was really surprised and amazed by that. And grateful.

> *SHELLY rises and holds out her arms, startling everyone.*

SHELLY (*calm, blissful*): I'm gonna have my baby right here.

> *PAUL gently pulls SHELLY back into her seat. The four eat in silence as lights fade.*

SCENE 2

That night. MARIAN pulls out the sofa bed. BETH enters from the bedroom with sheets and pillows.

SHELLY: We don't mind taking the couch.

MARIAN: No, no. This way you can have your privacy, to, you know, use the bathroom and what-have-you.

SHELLY: Well, if you're sure.

BETH: It's fine.

SHELLY: Thanks.

PAUL (O.S.): Babe? Where's my toothbrush?

SHELLY exits into the bedroom.

MARIAN: I'm just worried about your back.

BETH: Don't.

MARIAN: This bar in the middle won't—?

BETH: If it does, I'll move to the floor. Better for us to be here. Between them and the front door.

MARIAN: You're right. We better sleep in shifts.

BETH: Come on. Don't give me a hard time.

MARIAN: Then, admit it's nice.

BETH: What's nice?

MARIAN: Just... to know he's in the next room.

BETH: I just hope they don't get into any wild sexcapades in there.

MARIAN: What about us, out here?

BETH: Gee, you think there's a chance?

There is a knock at the front door. BETH opens it to NAT. She is sober now, and moves stiffly.

NAT: I see we still have company.

MARIAN: We thought... for tonight...

PAUL is heard laughing offstage.

NAT: I knew it.

MARIAN: Nat, I know I should have called—

NAT: This comes as no surprise to me. Didn't I say—?

BETH: Yes. You most certainly called it.

MARIAN: He's drug free now. And working. Nat, I know it's a lot to ask—

NAT: You're damn right.

MARIAN: Just until we can get them set up in a place. We need to find something cheap, alongside U.S. 1. Maybe a week? Two? You won't even know they're here. Unless... if you have anything around the house that needs fixing— Paul's working in pools. Your man hasn't been able to correct that algae problem. Maybe Paul can take a look.

NAT *(to Beth)*: Didn't you tell her what I said?

MARIAN: We haven't had much time—

BETH: I tried.

MARIAN: I know what you're wondering about. The arrest was for Assault. But it was an accident. And he was provoked.

NAT: How can it be both? I want them gone in the morning.

MARIAN: He'll do better this time.

NAT: Marian, I'm sorry for you. Truly. But this is a family matter, and frankly, I'm learning to appreciate the fact that I'm not actually a member of your family.

BETH: I never said—

MARIAN: No, Nat, I heard all about it. Beth wasn't shutting you out. She just wasn't sure what I'd want her to say to you. It's not your fault. It's ours. We should know each other better.

NAT: That's between the two of you.

MARIAN: I completely agree. Maybe some people don't take favors well—

BETH: Meaning me, I guess?

MARIAN: Meaning a lot of people. *(To Nat)* But you know we love you.

NAT: Do I?

MARIAN: Look in any crowd. Look at the people on any street corner. Can you point out which ones don't deserve to be loved? Why make yourself the one exception?

NAT: What the hell kind of hogwash— I don't agree with you, so I need my head shrunk, is that the deal?

MARIAN: I think it's the reason you're still alone.

NAT: You've got some big hairy nerve.

MARIAN: If we have to move the debt back onto our credit cards, to prove to you—

NAT: Listen, lady—

MARIAN: You don't want them here. I understand, and I don't blame you. I wouldn't even have asked if I didn't really believe he's so much better. Never mind, I'll talk to my pastor tomorrow, and I'm sure we can figure out something else. But Beth and I don't ever want to hear another word about you not being a very important and beloved part of this family.

NAT: Especially not when you need something.

MARIAN: I don't believe that's you talking. Why were you drinking so early today?

NAT: Gee, I wonder!

MARIAN: It wasn't Paul. You had a glass in your hand when we got home. Before his name was ever mentioned.

NAT: Well, that girl—

MARIAN: What? You came here and saw her, and went home and made yourself a drink?

BETH: Marian, leave it alone.

MARIAN: No, she told us to keep after her. For Heaven's sake, it was still morning. Tell me what you were thinking.

NAT: Seems stupid now.

MARIAN: What? What was it?

NAT: I was on the front porch when you two drove out on your donut run. I waved. You didn't wave back.

MARIAN: We must not have seen you.

NAT: I thought you did.

MARIAN: You're right, that does seem stupid. We would never pass by you without waving.

NAT: Maybe I was just feeling sorry for myself.

MARIAN: You promised you'd call me first, whenever you felt like starting early.

NAT: Listen, Beth, dolly, I'm sorry as hell.

BETH: It's okay.

NAT: I was drunk, and cranky and...

BETH: It's okay.

NAT: Here you are having a hideous time, and I'm just—

BETH: Don't think about it.

NAT: I used to be fun at parties. People used to come on to me.

MARIAN: I know, honey. Shhh...

PAUL (O.S.): Give that back, bitch!

SHELLY (O.S.): Come get it, bitch! Don't! You'll tear it! It's not mine!

Laughter is heard offstage.

MARIAN: Do you... want to see Paul? I think he'd like to see you before—

NAT: No! Not now.

NAT hurries to the door.

MARIAN: Will you let me walk you back?

NAT: No, doll, no.

MARIAN: I think I should.

NAT: You've got your hands full.

MARIAN: Well... I might be able to drag Paul to church tomorrow. You're welcome to come with us.

NAT: You know better than that. But... bring him over when you get back, to take a look.

MARIAN: What?

NAT: The algae. It's mostly by the steps, and around the drain.

MARIAN: You mean—?

NAT: We can take it one day at a time.

MARIAN: Bless you! You won't regret it! You're gonna see a big change!

> *MARIAN throws her arms around NAT.*

NAT: Alright, alright! Don't make me take a hose to you!

> *NAT exits. MARIAN waves her down the steps, then closes the door.*

BETH: We did see her wave this morning.

MARIAN: I wasn't about to tell her that.

> *MARIAN goes to the bedroom door and knocks.*

Paul? Are you decent? Hello?

> *PAUL sticks his head out of the bedroom. His face looks red and giggly from rough-housing.*

I just wanted to let you know your Aunt Nat was here.

PAUL: Where?

MARIAN: Was. She just left.

PAUL: Shucks. Wish I'd known. *(To Shelly, inside the bedroom)* Put that down. It's wet. Cut it out!

> *He laughs and plays a tug-of-war with SHELLY in the other room.*

BETH: Your mother is trying to talk to you.

> *PAUL comes out and closes the door.*

MARIAN: Nat said you can stay. I just thought you'd sleep better, knowing that. I know I will.

PAUL: Thanks.

MARIAN: But you have to behave yourself.

PAUL: Yeah, no problem. That it?

MARIAN: Yep. Pretty much.

BETH: Not quite.

PAUL: What else?

MARIAN: There's plenty of time—

BETH: Tell him the rest. I want to sleep better, too.

PAUL: What?

MARIAN: It's nothing. I told her you'd clean her pool. You can do that, can't you?

PAUL's smile suddenly fades.

PAUL: Yeah, we'll see.

MARIAN: We better see.

PAUL: I gotcha, mom.

BETH: It won't stop with cleaning the pool. She'll have you mowing the yard—

MARIAN: ...Don't make it sound like—

BETH: Taking out her recycling—

MARIAN: We never talked about recycling!

BETH: You gonna be okay with all that?

PAUL: We'll see.

MARIAN: We better see!

BETH: Have you thought for one minute about what's gonna happen tomorrow? And the next day? And the next?

PAUL: What do you think should happen?

MARIAN: He'll go to work.

BETH: Okay. Where is this job?

MARIAN: In Broward County.

BETH: How do you expect to get all the way up there every day? Answer me!

MARIAN: Tell her.

He doesn't answer.

This one guy he works with picks Paul up on U.S. 1 in the Grove, and leaves him back off. We can drop him off at U.S. 1 in the mornings. His boss... Charlie, wasn't it? Apparently very supportive. Which must mean he's doing a great job.

PAUL: Yeah, I can dig a hole with the best of 'em.

MARIAN: I'm sure there's more to it than that.

BETH: You pay taxes on this job?

PAUL: Off the books, babe.

BETH: Cash under the table. Come and go as you please.

MARIAN: He won't go anywhere. He likes his job.

PAUL: Yeah, the guys are great. And the clients. Fuckin' fantastic human specimens. Sittin' there drinkin' those tall glasses of iced tea in their air-conditioned living rooms, and starin' out their sliding glass doors, watchin' us busting our asses out in the hot sun for their entertainment and future luxury.

MARIAN: But Paul—

PAUL *(barreling on)*: What, they think we can't see through the glass right back at 'em? Watchin' us like fuckin' reality TV or some shit!

MARIAN: Hush!

PAUL: And not just the kids, but the mom, and the housekeeper, and they probably invite the neighbors, too, and I'm like, I ought to run this damn wheelbarrow right through the fuckin' glass!

MARIAN: Maybe they... think you're handsome.

                  PAUL laughs.

BETH: This isn't funny, Paul.

MARIAN: This is not how you were talking before.

BETH: I don't doubt it.

PAUL: Least I'm doin' my part for the man.

MARIAN: Stop it. You sound just like your father.

PAUL: Chip off the old shoulder, eh? One cliché begets another.

MARIAN: Why does everything you say have to be so loaded?

PAUL: Just tellin' it like it is, mom.

MARIAN: To be truly honest, you can only mean one thing at a time.

PAUL: Where do you get that? The Gay Baptist Almanac of Absolutes?

BETH: Marian, leave us alone.

MARIAN: No.

BETH: Go on. Now's a good time to take that laundry over.

PAUL: Go ahead, mom.

MARIAN: No.

PAUL: I want you to.

BETH: You owe me.

PAUL *(speaking into the bedroom)*: Babe, get that back on, and get those clothes together. I want you to go help my mom with the wash.

MARIAN: If we wash 'em tonight, we have to dry 'em tonight.

BETH: I'll go back over later if you don't want to wait up.

MARIAN: What are you going to say?

BETH: Trust me.

PAUL: It's alright, mom. She deserves equal time.

> *SHELLY enters with a pillow case full of dirty clothes. She and MARIAN exit. PAUL closes the door behind them and leans against it.*

We're all alone now. What is it? Money? You want me to pay it back?

BETH: Which money?

PAUL: ...

BETH: No. I'm not talking about money.

PAUL: Then I'm listening.

BETH: Just about every Saturday for more than a year, your mother and I went for a "drive." Looking in different neighborhoods, all over town. Asking in English, Spanish, French... "Have you seen this man?" Coming home hot, tired and empty-handed.

PAUL: A year? Shoulda stopped earlier.

BETH: The only thing more painful than those Saturdays were the Saturdays that followed. When we didn't go. When we didn't look. And the Sundays when your mother couldn't get herself up to go to church. I thought she might never go again.

PAUL: What a shame.

BETH: It's what keeps her going.

PAUL: In other words, y'all missed me. Thanks.

BETH: I just have one thing to say.

PAUL: Just one?

BETH: Pretty simple.

PAUL: Lemme guess. Those "three little words?"

> *BETH doesn't respond. PAUL lets out an awkward guffaw.*

BETH: Just stay in line. That's all. Take responsibility for this charge. The price now is as small as it'll get.

PAUL: Talk about prices, why don't you ask the big money question?

BETH: Your mother—

PAUL: Thinks I couldn't hurt a fly. But you want details, don't you? How I put the hurt on old Hernandez.

BETH: I want you to LISTEN, God damn it!

PAUL: Whoa! Fightin' words. Aren't you scared I'll bounce you off the furniture?

BETH: I'm not afraid of you. Or challenged, or upset, or disappointed, like your mother. In fact, maybe I'm just a little bored.

PAUL: Nice front.

BETH: Oh, I promise you. One false step and you'll be back in that jail cell before you knew what hit you.

PAUL: Just what you're hoping for, I bet.

BETH: You're wrong. I'm hoping you'll do the right thing, the responsible thing, for once. See this through, Paul. If you don't, I guarantee you, your mother will never get over it.

PAUL: How about you?

BETH: Just, I'll respect you for doing the right thing.

PAUL: For my mom's sake.

BETH: And your own, whether you'll believe it or not.

PAUL: But you—

BETH: I'm just here for— I'm just here.

PAUL: Just here. Just here. What are you, a potted plant?

> *BETH involuntarily backs away.*

Oh. It moves.

BETH: Paul.

PAUL: No, I think you'd look better in that corner.

BETH: Paul.

> *He moves toward her. BETH takes a few steps toward the door.*

PAUL: It's walking AND talking. Have I gone crazy? No, I don't think it goes there. It really needs to be put in its proper place.

> *PAUL moves her around by the shoulders.*

BETH: Paul! My back!

PAUL: The hip bone's connected to the—

> *PAUL shoves BETH against the wall.*

Now that's what I call art!

BETH: Put me down!

PAUL: God, Beth, you can't take a joke anymore.

> *He releases her. She moves away. He paces, then bursts forth and throws his arms around her, erupting in sobs. BETH stands rigid to the embrace, but gradually returns it somewhat. MARIAN and SHELLY enter.*
>
> *MARIAN's initial shock turns to a mixture of joy and jealousy. As she approaches to join them, BETH pulls away from PAUL. He watches her, avoiding Marian's embrace for a second time.*

BETH: I can't stay here with him.

MARIAN: What?

BETH: I can't.

PAUL: You don't have to. We're leavin'!

MARIAN: No!

PAUL: Shelly, get our stuff!

SHELLY: No!

PAUL: I said, "Get our stuff!"

SHELLY: I just had our stuff! I just put our stuff in a washing machine, you asshole!

PAUL: Don't worry, we're gonna go get it.

MARIAN: Paul, no!

SHELLY: It's all soaked.

PAUL *(to Shelly)*: Get our backpacks! Let's go!

SHELLY: Don't yell at me, dickwad!

> *SHELLY stalks into the bedroom.*

MARIAN: You can't miss your court date!

PAUL: Don't you get it?!

MARIAN: You won't go to jail! We'll hire a real lawyer! We'll prove it was an accident!

PAUL: That shit was no accident. It was me. Mr. Fuckup. In the parking lot. With a barrel tile. Game over.

MARIAN: You're just upset. Don't let Beth—

PAUL: I wanted to lay ol' Hernandez out so she wouldn't get back up. But she moved her arms too much. Couldn't get good purchase.

BETH: That's enough!

PAUL: And I got some left over for that bitch up front, keepin' you guys prisoner back here, and tryin' to rape my girlfriend and turn me into a fuckin' slave!

MARIAN: Don't you dare hurt anyone!

> *PAUL storms into the bedroom. BETH hurries to the phone and dials.*

BETH: Nat. Lock your doors and call 911. Do it!

> *PAUL enters with his backpack. BETH hangs up.*

The cops are on the way.

> *PAUL stares at BETH, then laughs aloud.*

PAUL *(to Shelly, offstage)*: Step on it, babe, or we'll have an escort.

> *SHELLY hurries out with her backpack, stuffing toiletries in it.*

SHELLY *(to Marian)*: I'm borrowing this moisturizer. I hope you don't mind. It has sunblock. Oh, wait!

> *SHELLY unplugs her cell phone and packs it in her bag.*

PAUL: Oh, yeah, can't forget that. Okay, now...

> *PAUL scans the room for MARIAN's purse. Marian glances toward the kitchen sink. Paul starts toward it. Marian runs past him and stands in front of the cabinet.*

Get outta the way.

MARIAN: Don't do this.

PAUL: Don't make me hurt you.

MARIAN: You wouldn't.

> *PAUL lunges toward her. She shrinks away.*

> *He gets MARIAN's purse. Marian pounds on his back. He laughs.*

Why are you doing this to me?!! How can you do this to me?!

PAUL: How can I? Do this to you?

MARIAN: What???! What have I done?! TELL ME!!! TELL ME!!!

> *She slaps at him. He takes it.*

SHELLY: Don't make him mad!

BETH: Let him go! We can't stop him.

> *PAUL fishes out MARIAN's keys. He tosses the wallet to SHELLY. She removes the cash and hands the wallet to Marian.*

SHELLY: I know what a drag it is to get a new license and everything. Hey, you'll never get anything out of him. But basically it boils down to, you know, just don't let your conscience bother you. Well? If we're going, let's go!

> *SHELLY performs a curtsey for MARIAN, shoots a last look at BETH, then exits. PAUL heads for the door.*

BETH: Leave Nat alone. You don't have time.

PAUL: She ain't worth my time. Sorry about the car, but you'da lost it anyway, right?

> *PAUL exits. BETH dials.*

BETH: Hey. They just left here. Did you call? ...Good. Looks like they're not stopping. See you in a minute.

> *BETH watches out the door.*

SFX: A CAR PEELS OUT

They didn't stop. Thank God.

MARIAN: God had nothing to do with this.

> *They stare at each other for a long time. BETH breaks away first and puts on her jeans. MARIAN goes into the bedroom. Beth sits at the table and starts to write something on a piece of paper. Marian enters wearing street clothes.*

> ### *SFX: SIRENS*

> *Sirens are heard approaching, and then red lights flash in the windows. The women go to the door as lights fade.*

SCENE 3

Later that night. BETH and MARIAN enter. Beth folds a copy of a police report and puts it on a shelf. Marian starts to un-make the sofa bed.

BETH: I'll do this. Take some Nyquil or something. Just go in and try to go to sleep.

> *MARIAN moves away from the sofa. BETH folds up the bed and starts putting the cushions back to restore the sofa.*

MARIAN: So full of hate. Women.

BETH: Come on. Try not to think about it right now.

MARIAN: Is it because—?

BETH: There's no because. Please hush and go lie down.

MARIAN: I've been so selfish! We must have—!

BETH: We nothing. Please. Go lie down. I'll be in soon.

MARIAN: We destroyed him.

BETH: Okay, then sit down. You need to hear this. Maybe I should have told you a long time ago, I don't know...

> *BETH sits MARIAN on the half-restored sofa and holds her hands as she speaks.*

When you were visiting your aunt, and I took Paul on that "bonding trip", to Key West, remember? Before I ever moved in with you. This was before we were officially a "we." There was a little girl sitting across from us on the trolley. She'd been attacked at some point by a dog or something. Her face was kinda marred. Marian... Paul threw a penny at her and called her "scarface."

MARIAN: Oh! Don't.

BETH: She pretended not to hear him. She was with some adults, maybe her grandparents, but Paul was careful to say it only loud enough for her. I pinched him. He said it again. I pinched him again. Then he said it three times in a row, real quick. "Scarface, scarface, scarface." I grabbed his wrist and yanked him out of his seat and dragged him up the aisle. Just to get him away from her. She never moved, just kept staring. I'll never forget the way he laughed. That was before we were a "we." He was already like that. Laughing the way he did tonight. The same laugh.

MARIAN: What did you do about it?

BETH: I didn't know what to do.

MARIAN: Scold him? Correct him?

BETH: If I did, it was no use. When we got to Southernmost Point, Paul forgot all about that girl. He was thrilled with the lighthouse, and the ocean, and the boats.

BETH (CONT'D): We stood with our backs to the land and looked out at the nothing. Paul said if he had a slingshot, he'd knock the cigar out of Castro's mouth. He was so full of fight. Smiling up at me. Daring me to admit that seeing him have a good time was not what I wanted most in life.

MARIAN: So that's where the battle of wills started.

BETH: Wills? I don't know. No. I think that's where I lost mine. Southernmost Point is how I feel every time I look at Paul, or hear his name. The world at my back. Staring out at nothing. Feeling nothing. Learning to hope for nothing.

        MARIAN pulls her hands away.

MARIAN: You never loved him at all, did you?

BETH: I was always there. I've stuck by you, through—

MARIAN: By ME!

BETH: Huh?

MARIAN: You stuck by ME. I watched you tell that boy when he was ten years old, that you loved HIM and would always be there for him. ALWAYS, you said. You made him a promise. At an age where he knew what it meant, and needed desperately to believe it.

BETH: I was young. But I kept my promise!

MARIAN: No! You abandoned him, too! And worse! You stayed around to be a constant reminder!

BETH: So now it wasn't we, it was me? Don't do this now. Let's just stop talking.

MARIAN: You chased him out of here today!

BETH: Oh, yeah, I was really desperate to lose that pesky vehicle!

MARIAN: You picked a fight with Nat so he couldn't stay, traumatized his girlfriend, and goaded him—

BETH: Stop it!

MARIAN: —from the minute he walked through the door!

BETH: Which you promised me he would not be doing!

MARIAN: Then punish me, not him!

BETH: You'd do anything— say anything to escape the simple, simple truth! That your body produced something defective!

MARIAN: And you can't accept the fact that your body produced nothing at all!

        A long pause.

BETH: Nothing? Yeah. That's right.

MARIAN: Honey...

BETH: No. Yeah. You're right. I've produced nothing.

BETH goes into the bedroom. MARIAN falls to the couch, stunned. Beth enters with a handful of clothes draped over her shoulder. She plops them on the back of the couch. Beth goes back in the bedroom, and comes in again with toiletry items. Then she gets an overnight bag, and opens it out on the kitchen counter.

MARIAN: Beth. Please. Honey... What are you doing?

BETH packs the overnight bag.

BETH: Once we stopped looking for Paul, what was left? Saturday morning donuts?

MARIAN: I said a stupid, vicious thing. I'm sorry.

BETH: At least that was the truth. I watched you lie to Nat. Outright lie to her. I told myself you were desperate. Didn't know what you were doing. You knew.

MARIAN: It would be cruel to tell her the truth.

BETH: Instead, you told her the lies she wanted to hear. And cajoled her. And flattered her. And it worked.

MARIAN: Yes. And she felt a hundred times better. After your version of "the truth" today, she was ready to slit her wrists.

BETH: At least she could make up her own mind how to really feel.

MARIAN: I made her really feel happy. Loved. And I'm prepared to back up whatever I said, no matter what it takes, 'til the day one of us dies.

BETH: Is that what you expected me to do with Paul? ...Is that what you've been doing with me? All the time I've been protecting you, indulging you, making excuses—

MARIAN: I've cared for you!

BETH: You've manipulated me— all of us— for so long—

MARIAN: And look where it's got me. How good at it can I be?

BETH starts for the door.

You tell me the same kind of lies.

BETH: Such as?

MARIAN: You say you respect my belief in God.

BETH: That's right.

MARIAN: No. You tolerate it. Barely. To yourself, you laugh at my prayers. You feel superior the rest of the day.

BETH: Because you don't just believe in God, you believe everything!

MARIAN: Somebody has to!

BETH: I believed something once.

MARIAN: What?

BETH: That somebody on this earth could really be as good as you seemed.

MARIAN: Beth...

BETH: For that, I gave up ever having my own kid, because yours needed so, so much attention. And when it still doesn't turn out the way you wanted, which it never could, you throw my sacrifice in my face. I don't know much about religion, but I don't think that's considered Christian.

BETH reaches the door.

MARIAN: I can't be alone tonight!

BETH: Go over to Nat's.

MARIAN: She might have already left. She's so freaked out, she's checking into a hotel. I told her there was no need.

BETH: Maybe she'll meet someone in the lobby.

MARIAN: Beth... We already did the hard part. We shouldn't have to grow old alone. There's got to be something left. Something that we had to push aside, maybe. Or push down, just to get through things.

BETH throws her bag over her shoulder.

I know it's hard to remember, because Paul was always there. But there was a time when we couldn't keep our hands to ourselves.

BETH: We got over that.

MARIAN: You never know.

BETH turns to look MARIAN full in the face. Marian kisses Beth.

BETH: How do I know this isn't another manipulation?

MARIAN: As long as you're getting what you really want, does it matter?

BETH: What I really want is truth.

MARIAN: I know. And I've spent the last twenty years trying to create it for you. Isn't that what love is?

BETH: Not to me.

MARIAN: It's like, Faith. You try to live by the Word because you value it. Without proof. You give your life to it. Even though, there are times when you want to just... So you use the word, Love, and you know you want that to be what it is. What you feel. And you want that so much, that you never stop saying it. Or playing it out.

BETH: Love is an extremely consistent lie. That's what you're telling me.

MARIAN: No. What I mean is... if you never stop wanting to try... that's the proof.

BETH ponders this, then starts out.

Alright! The truth. You want me to say the truth. That I know. Because I must—I do. I know.

BETH comes back into the doorway, staring at MARIAN with a mixture of anticipation and horror. Marian can barely wrench the words from her gut.

MARIAN (CONT'D): He is, I know he is, I can't, but I do, I always have known, he's... our son, he's... broken, isn't he, he's broken and he's never, he's never gonna—

BETH drops her bag and puts a hand over MARIAN's mouth. Marian falls silent, grateful. Beth takes Marian in her arms.

NAT (O.S.): Yoo hoo. Marian? Beth?

NAT appears in the doorway. Registering the fragile moment, she remains respectfully quiet, but remains. After a moment...

BETH: We thought you checked into a hotel.

NAT: What, the Straightjacket Arms? I'd hafta be crazy to leave my gals at a time like this. And Bonnie and Clyde would be even crazier to come back here. Be outta state by morning.

MARIAN gasps back a sob.

Besides. Those bedbug warnings you hear every time you turn around lately. Thank you muchly, but no thank you. I'm good. We're good. Right here.

NAT joins the hug as lights very slowly fade.

END OF PLAY

ABOUT STAGE RIGHTS

Based in Los Angeles and founded in 2000, Stage Rights is one of the foremost independent theatrical publishers in the United States, providing stage performance rights for a wide range of plays and musicals to theater companies, schools, and other producing organizations across the country and internationally. As a licensing agent, Stage Rights is committed to providing each producer the tools they need for financial and artistic success. Stage Rights is dedicated to the future of live theatre, offering special programs that champion new theatrical works.

To view all of our current plays and musicals, visit:

www.stagerights.com

44736436R00034

Made in the USA
Middletown, DE
15 June 2017